Dr. Tracy Sainvil-Joslyn

Teacher to Teacher

How Tenured Teachers and Self-Evaluation Leads to Success in the Classroom

Published by Dr. Tracy Sainvil-Joslyn
PO Box 27027
Philadelphia, PA 19118

Cover design and page formatting: Lisa Pearson
Cover photo courtesy of SDI Productions for Unsplash

Acknowledgements

To life and its many blessings.

Giving many thanks to those that came before me and those coming after.

I would like to acknowledge my husband Jah Evans and my Joslyn 5: Jah'Seek'I, Jah'Seek'He, Jah'Mosi, N'Yahme, and Taitu. They've been and continue to be my all-time cheerleaders. To my loving mother who has always had big dreams for me.

I am grateful for being able to develop this work as a Rastafarian woman guided by the principles of Ma'at.

Thank you to Ms. Lisa Pearson for your thought partnership and listening ear during my writing journey.

Lastly, I'd like to acknowledge every hardworking educator and school leader that I've had the privilege to work with, mentor, learn from, and inspire. Being an educator is heart-work. To those that had or still have the heart to do the great work of teaching, leading, and caring, I personally thank you. Giving many thanks for your endearing support.

Peace and Blessings,
Dr. Tracy

Table of Contents

The Catalyst

☑

The Catalyst

To be honest with you, this is the book I wish I had when I began my teaching career. Over the years, there have been lots of potholes and obstacles that I've managed to overcome, but there was a specific time period that changed everything. Here is a brief excerpt from my dissertation written in 2021 that summarizes some of my experience:

> For the past four years, teaching in an urban public school, I have been grappling with balancing my instructional duties as well as the daily administrative tasks. The load of work became too heavy to bear, making me feel as if I was inadequate. With over 17 years in education I found myself with feelings of doubts on the kind of impact that I was really making with students. My principals "did their best" to conduct evaluations in a fair manner but that wasn't

my reality. I quickly learned that if I had too much to say in response to an evaluation that I would risk scrutiny or reprimand by my administrators. If it wasn't for my firm belief that education can help children overcome adversities, as well as the fact that children need great teachers, then I would've left in the middle of last year. I had had enough. I know my abilities to impact my students were there but I didn't understand "What made me stay in a profession that is emotionally, physically, spiritually, and mentally abusive?" After many conversations with various staff, friends, and families I started believing that I was truly endowed to be a teacher and that the students needed someone like me. What I couldn't figure out was how would a teacher with as many years experience as me be able to feel positive about teaching if they truly felt ill-equipped in the 21st century classroom.

The truth is, new and veteran teachers are likely always trying to stay abreast of the constantly shifting teaching landscape. But many were just trying to survive amidst the shadows of the COVID-19 pandemic (2020-present). Educators and school leaders across the nation are diligently working to recoup time lost from education in the last two years. Particularly facing greater hardship are educators in large urban school districts who face different challenges, teachers who teach marginalized groups of youths, including children of African descent, and children whose first language is not English. Specifically targeted in this book are educators and school leaders in large underfunded public schools and *Additional Targeted Support and Improvement* Schools or A-TSI Schools.

A-TSI Schools are "schools in which performance by one or more student groups is at or below the level of the Comprehensive Support and Improvement (CSI) Schools." It's a fancy name for underperforming schools that don't have much but need a lot. It indicates school failure and/or lacking significant progress.

These are the conditions that add to or raise the responsibilities that educators face. As a novice educator in the A-TSI Schools, there are adjustments that must be made. On top of being responsible for human beings, developing a teaching style, and understanding when to show grace for the children, our colleagues, and ourselves, the novice teacher must learn how to navigate a school without resources. At some point they may ask "I tried this but it didn't work. Now what?"

While that is common in the teaching experience, it is different for the teacher in the A-TSI School. There's a big transition in going from book learning (theory) into the hands-on human factor and on-the-job training (application) of navigating children and surviving administrators or colleagues who may or may not help. And sometimes, there's no one to ask, *Now what?* because the reality is that there are not enough assigned mentors to ask. Why? Underfunding also means mentorship inequity in certain districts.

Veteran tenured teachers in the same schools are also forced to ratchet up their survival skills. It's hard to be a teacher for ten, fifteen, even thirty years and be met with a change in administration or even teaching curriculum. Common Core followed by the conversion to online learning during the Covid-19 pandemic was traumatic for some. Some lunged at the chance to retire or resign from a profession they loved. At the same time, some had the foresight to rely on the novice teachers who had a better grasp on technology.

In what I perceived as the worst year of my life, I was "graced" with a new administrator. He did not take to me. He immediately identified me as a teacher who was going to give him problems - meaning I would ask the uncomfortable questions and ask for what I needed despite the limitations that had already been laid out. In addition, I was assigned to a new grade and content specialty. Not only was it a new grade, but I got "the class" which most teachers understood to be the most challenging class to have in the whole building! Also, it was a testing grade which means there were standardized/state assessments that the children had to be prepared for in addition to their regular curriculum. As a veteran teacher all these "news" were overwhelming. I researched what I didn't understand, but I still needed materials. I had books from 1990. I needed training. I did not want to be set up for failure. For many school-based reasons I was also denied attending training and things I wanted to purchase because my subject didn't have a curriculum. Typically, only English and Math have a curriculum in the state of Pennsylvania. Science curriculum varies from school to school. When faced with these obstacles, the teacher compiles information here and there. Or does nothing.

I had no resources, no administrative support, and the children had extreme behavioral support needs which impacted instruction and learning. I was a veteran teacher facing a mountain of "new" with no one to offer me hiking boots, a compass, or a map. Yet still, doing nothing was not an option. I had to remember that I come from a legacy of leaders, activists, educators, and freedom fighters. It was at that moment where I came to a final stance. I would have to use my aptitude and experience to ensure that the educational philosophy I have on student learning and achievement doesn't shift. I would make it my duty to examine the role of a teacher through an administrative lens. This angle of study allowed me to know what things I had to do on my own. More importantly, it revealed how effective feedback from administrators can greatly influence and impact educator success.

In the summer of that year, in determining my Ph.D. topic, I had a burgeoning question that bubbled up from my personal difficulties. How do teachers persevere through adversity? I did everything to not fail that year. I was of the belief that this administrator sat by and thought, *Let me see how she does this without resources.* Spoiler: I did well. It was evident on the day that the Administrator brought me the test scores in amazement. The results showed that 56 out of 68 students (more than 80% of my students) made gains while 44% were proficient or advanced that year. The bridge between us started being repaired in that moment of acknowledgement. The administrator and I had personal issues, but that could not trump the instruction the children received or the proof of the test scores. The administrator acknowledged that the perseverance, commitment, and dedication to succeed with students in the classroom led to gains unexpected from an under-resourced environment. It may seem a simple thing, but that acknowledgment eased the feeling of being underestimated as one who is effective in helping the children grow and mislabeled as a problem teacher. And this, teacher friends, is how my dissertation topic evolved.

I began my research after hitting that rough patch in my teaching career. This career, which is supposed to equip our children to face and run the world in the very near future, was like an emotionally, physically, spiritually, and mentally abusive relationship. I felt drained of hope and beaten down, could never give enough, and had no support. And then I doubted myself. The pain was overwhelming. And yet, I stayed. What made me stay? The short answer: Learning that I had the ability and the confidence in my ability to teach. The shorter answer: The children.

I've since deduced that success in the classroom is about hitting the goal of achievement in the children and a desired professional outcome for the teacher. However, the goal gets pretty cloudy when feelings of inadequacy begin to surface.

New teachers seek nurturing, like newborns and toddlers do. They need help walking in the big responsibility of caring for children. They want very much to do it on their own but they haven't quite gotten their balance. Some voices around them say, *Figure it out,* while others say, *Don't worry about getting your balance. All you have to do here is show up.* Neither of these options are truly helpful.

On the other hand, veteran teachers need internal and external reassurance in the form of feedback. They need help with the new technology and the new generation who cause feelings of ineffectiveness to arise. That is, unless they are the lifetime-student-type always looking for a way to improve.

In case you were wondering, that's who this book is for: the new teacher who wants to walk confidently but needs guidance. And the veteran teacher who just figured out the DVD player and wants to learn how to work that new [smart phone, tablet, app]. This book is for the lifetime student who knows there is always something new to learn or something to reassess in order to achieve greater impact in the world. It's also for the teacher whose evaluations haven't quite helped them get better, but rather deflated their sense of effectiveness in the classroom.

Lastly, this book is for school and district leaders who desire to understand and weave together the research, best practices, and educator feedback as it relates to educator effectiveness and evaluations. In other words, this is for the one who desires to measure and improve their self-efficacy.

This book is designed to help you build the courage to challenge your level of self-efficacy as an educator and school leader. Educators with higher levels of efficacy in domain specific tasks are driven to find solutions for improving the educational outcomes of their learners, are committed to educational equity and justice, and are effective in sustaining an efficacious educator mindset (Sainvil-Joslyn, 2021).

Newness and changes are inevitable in teaching. My aim is to help you remain grounded in your abilities and sure of your effectiveness as an educator. It will take some work, but if you're reading, I am sure you are ready for it.

Cheers to becoming better teachers and teaching children well.

Let's win this together.

The Discovery of Self-Efficacy

Chapter 1
What is Self-Efficacy?

So HOW WOULD A TEACHER with many years of experience be able to feel positive about teaching if they felt ill-equipped? How would they persevere through adversity? The answer to how I finally came to a good place evolved from my research. There was, of course, the insight of tenured teachers and some cheerleading. However, I also needed something that would last when the cheering and motivational push of others was not available. For me, there was an evaluative process that provided the reinforcement of the belief that I had the ability and the confidence in my ability to teach. In other words, I learned self-efficacy and how to evaluate self-efficacy (the identification of one's abilities and the mental fortitude to draw on the knowledge and certainty of that ability at all times) to ensure student achievement and outcomes.

The research was personal to me. I had to find a way to encourage myself and others around me for the long haul. I knew that I had ability. The kids' test scores affirmed that. But the confidence in the ability would wane when met with the resistance that I described in my worst year ever and even with personal life events. Teaching is one of those jobs that requires one to show up. But showing up is subject to outside factors that can interrupt the inner parts of the teacher who must be fully present and engaged for the children.

I learned that I needed to evaluate myself. I also needed to learn how those with shared life experiences, race, and culture managed. That evaluation came through my research of how to persevere. I had to look (and evaluate) within. For this monumental task, I utilized something some of you may be familiar with: the Danielson Framework for Teaching and the Bandura Model for Self-Efficacy which I showcase below.

The Danielson Framework for Teaching (FFT)

Here's a brief recap of the Danielson timeline from my dissertation:

In 1996, Charlotte Danielson published The Framework for Teaching as a method for promoting authentic conversations about teaching practices between educators and school leaders. The Framework is a "comprehensive approach to teacher professional learning across the career continuum-from pre-service teacher preparation through teacher leadership" (Danielson, 2013). There are four domains and twenty-two components, within this comprehensive Framework, used during formal and informal classroom observations and feedback sessions to promote student learning. With these parameters, school leaders can decide to create meaningful conversations centered on teaching and learning or use it to assess perceived observations of teaching practices."

In 2013, the Framework for Teaching was updated to include additional expectations interpreted through "specific rubric language, critical attributes, and teaching and learning in the context of the Common Core" (Danielson Group, 2013, p. 1). This updated edition presented a common language for teachers to voice the complex work involved in teaching. The updated version added a way for teachers and school leaders to share and reflect thoughts about the instruction before, during, and after an observation. I believe it is during the dialogic engagement between school leaders and teachers that factors, such as self-efficacy within domains, could be discussed to mitigate barriers towards achieving ratings that demonstrate effective teaching performance. Understanding teacher self-efficacy within Danielson's Framework for Effective Teaching evaluation tool can give school leaders more insight on improving the organization through accelerating and sharing best teacher practices and supporting emerging teachers in their need-specific area of growth (Sainvil-Joslyn, 2021).

As an educational leader I can commend the Danielson

group for updating the Framework to reflect the last couple of years of the Covid-19 pandemic's effect. The updates include an online tool that allows users to interact with each of the domains, gaining a more in-depth understanding. More than ever, educators and staff in larger urban public schools are facing budgetary, staffing, and mental health and wellness of students and staff.

Bandura Recap

Okay, so now let me demonstrate to you what Bandura (1993) identifies as the four processes that influence [teacher] behavior, in terms of self-efficacy.

Bandura's Four Processes that Influences Behavior

Processes	Characteristics or Attributes of Effectiveness
Cognitive	• Higher Self-Efficacy • Adopting Higher Goals • Increased Goal Commitment • Expectations goals will be achieved despite adversity
Motivational	• Self-Efficacy is linked to attribution theory • Outcome expectancies • Cognized goals-present rather than unforeseen future results
Affective	• Use of stress-reducing coping strategies • Higher resiliency with daily pressures • Greater career satisfaction
Selection	• Self-efficacy is influenced by the selection of activities and environments • Higher commitment to teaching

Self-Efficacy and the Models

From these models, I learned I had a very high level of self-efficacy, I believed that I could teach in the most challenging of circumstances, and more importantly, my profession was/is a very valuable asset in my life. This means I had to understand the evaluation tool (Danielson Framework for Teaching) that was used to measure my level of proficiency. Whether or not the evaluation process was conducted in a "fair" way was not a determinant for how I evaluated myself.

I learned that I had to figure out what mattered to me in my profession, how I was going to use the resources (including frameworks and models) around me to be better at my profession and what were the instruments being used to measure my performance.

In my case, the children's test scores reflected my ability and forced the administrator to back off. Not only did I get support from veteran teachers, I received encouragement from friends and family. But that was that year and those scholars. The next group of scholars in the following year(s) might test higher or lower depending on various circumstances. The question remained: what would I do when I didn't have family and friend support? I needed another method to evaluate. Upon understanding that self-efficacy (Bandura, 1977) was what some of my predecessors used to be resilient educators, I found surety in my abilities to use the Danielson Framework to enhance my evaluation skills. But my research would delve deeper than my own experience. I utilized the experience of veteran teachers because I wanted to learn if this was just something beneficial to me. This research was personal to me because the changes that I would experience would affect not only me, but other teachers, and most importantly, the children. I was concerned about the community-at-large.

There is pressure to perform in the world of an educator. Teachers still need to know they are effective and that the ethical oath that they took is in effect everyday. We can break under some of these pressures, especially when feelings of inadequacy creep in. If teachers explore the areas of inadequacy and learn their ability is present, there will come the healing that will benefit the children. The evaluation, believe it or not, helps us to work out a work-life balance where you get yourself together outside, so you don't bring it inside to the kids. When a teacher examines and does the work on finding the root cause of the feelings of inadequacy, the teacher will be more certain of their ability and will better be able to meet the goal of children achieving and closing the education gap. The education gap is widened by the poor conditions of the schools, the lack of current textbooks, and access to current technology. Furthermore, every day in America there are children going to school forced to survive the systematic racism of underfunded school buildings with inadequate resources. Inadequate resources lead to an increased need for teacher self-efficacy development. Frankly, it's oppressive not just to the students, but the teachers, too. Racism in education isn't a new strategy of oppression. Urban education deals with the recognition of racist and oppressive practices negatively impacting children of African descent and other ethnic groups of color. Racism in the urban educational system has called for the need for educational reform in teacher recruitment and development, high-stakes assessments, and zero-tolerance policies that limit access to students of African descent (Johnson, Boyden & Pittz, 2001).

My Mission

With this discovery, my mission is to get each educator, especially our tenured veteran teacher, to the place where they understand their level of self-efficacy within the context of an evaluation framework. Evaluation frameworks are developed for a number of accountability reasons. What's important is that each educator (in or out the classroom) that is being evaluated, teaching our most beloved and vulnerable populations of youths in large urban school districts, should be clear on what is expected of them, what they should expect for themselves as proficient and distinguished educators, and how it matters to kids. With the self-evaluation, the educator will even be able to identify and come to terms with the understanding that they can't or don't want to do this anymore. Maybe the educator is retiring. Great. But they still have the kids now. It's not over until it's over. I want to be a voice crying out to young teachers and veteran teachers facing the days/seasons of doubt. You have the ability. You can be confident in your ability. You will need to evaluate what they are or aren't so you can persevere, encourage yourself, and thrive in a way that will compel you to aid a younger teacher (like you once were) in their journey of educating the youth.

Why Focus on Evaluation Methods?

In this book, I am focused on the evaluation in terms of developing self-efficacy, as a conversation, rather than a tool to point out flaws. The evaluation is to be reframed as a tool that helps the teacher understand their strengths, discover and work on their weaknesses, and gain or reclaim the confidence to positively impact the children's achievement.

Evaluation methods can shape the teacher into who the students need. It can shape the teacher as a person and professional, too. The problem is that regular admin/teacher evaluations have different expectations, are usually a one-sided 45 minute observation, various methodologies are employed, and they can be biased. Although they are supposed to be objective, evaluations can be highly subjective.

Evaluations when done correctly and objectively can provide valuable feedback and insight into where an often transferable strength can be better utilized. At some points evaluations can be subjective, which is both good and bad. The good side is that it takes into consideration the extenuating circumstances unique to a classroom. On the bad side, information can be reviewed out of context without prior or post knowledge of the proper context. I will share a narrative of how this plays out later.

Evaluation Research Focus

My research focused "on the individual teaching stories that tenured veteran teachers self-reported." Their narratives helped to me to discover:

- how The Framework for Teaching (Danielson, 2013) should or should not be used,
- how to improve the quality of teacher pedagogy so that all learners are learning, and
- how to include teachers' voices so that district leaders can broaden their understanding, which includes eradicating misconceptions, on why some educators have higher self-efficacy than others who also teach in urban communities.

Evaluation of self-efficacy can have an effect on evaluation as a whole while it has an effect on other teachers, especially when veteran teachers share what they've learned with the younger. It becomes collaborative efficacy. It's a win-win for the student, teacher, administrator, school district, community, state, region, and the country. Does this sound like some kind of Utopian world? Probably. But as cliche as it sounds, change starts with one. And you're that one.

In those difficult days, the one thing I was sure of was that education could help the children overcome adversity. That was the reason I did not walk out on the students in the middle of the year. Neither did I see myself just coming in everyday for a check.

Let's face it, like most professions, there are those who care about the work they do and the people they serve in that line of work. Then there are those who come in to get a paycheck. Their performance ranges from the bare minimum to average to excellent. In teaching, there are children and, thus, communities that pay the price for the check-collectors of the world. To be fair, these are sometimes people who have lost hope due to lack of support or hardship both in and outside of the school building. I've been there. If that's you, it's time to level up. If leveling up is not something you desire, it's time to find a new profession. Not every educator is an educator to (younger) children. That can be remedied by moving to a higher grade or moving into post-secondary education. Apathy is contagious and affects both students and other teachers alike. And so for every one of us who desire for the children we've been entrusted with to meet their learning goals and achieve, we have work to do.

As we begin to explore the purpose of the efficacy evaluations, you will begin to see the picture of what that work entails.

The Self-Efficacy Evaluation Model in Education

The journey of collaboration is a personal one. What I mean by that is anytime that one professional takes the time to collaborate with another for the sake of evaluating skills for the purpose of improving then that's a step in positive outcomes for our students. However, being able to self-rate where you measure in levels of teacher self-efficacy is priceless professional development.

Similarly, the approach used for teacher reflection and self-evaluation is a personal one. In my Joslyn Teacher Self-Efficacy Scale 2021, an educator can self-rate through a reflective evaluative lens. At the point of merging those personal reflections with your professional ones you are moving your capacity to be efficacious in your pedagogy, leadership, and responsibility as an educator. Through the research and all the folks that impacted it, I was able to understand the core of how teacher self-efficacy can evolve for the positive.

The Self-Efficacy tool that I developed was adapted from Bandura's (2006) Teacher Self-Efficacy Scale and from meaningful thoughts and experiences. I wanted my self-efficacy tool to take into account efficacy perspectives that are specific to the evaluation process used in large urban school districts, particularly the Danielson Framework for Teaching. I included domain specific performance indicators and identified the domains that coincided with Bandura's (2006) original six efficacy categories.

The Self-Efficacy tool that I developed for my study can be used to support school leaders in making decisions for their educators and staff. It will assist leaders in understanding the ecological environment and functional areas that veteran educators need the most support or excel in; "using evaluation tools, that generalize teaching situations into structured competencies, should consider the social environment and its impact on a teachers' sense of efficacy within various contexts of a school day" (Sainvil-Joslyn, 2021, p. 46).

☑

Chapter 2
Self-Efficacy Factors

Self-Efficacy and Affirmations

These days, affirmations are very popular. It seems the world has caught on to the idea that positive self-talk and self-motivation are effective tools to achieving one's personal and professional goals; skillset and education notwithstanding. Affirmations can be of actual goals or they may be a feel-good tool for the wishful thinker. One may say, *I can do anything. I can build a rocket ship if I want to.* First, one must want to. Secondly, if one has no desire to seek the knowledge of how to build a rocket ship, be it by the study of physics, engineering, aerodynamics, or even watching YouTube videos, one most likely will not, no matter the affirmations, be able to build a rocket ship. Delusion is real. However, my research confirms that if you believe you are confident in your evaluated and confirmed abilities, you will have greater success. Affirmations can be as simple as:

- "I trust my ability to impact the children."
- "I am an expert at my subject matter."
- "I can grasp new concepts related to my subject matter."
- "I can relay this information in ways my students under-stand."

Again, self-efficacy is the identification of one's abilities through evaluative methods, and the mental fortitude to draw on the knowledge and certainty of that ability at all times. Affirmations quickly reassure and replenish the efficacy tank when doubt attempts to deplete it.

Self-Efficacy and Race

Working in an urban public school system as an educator of African descent, I believe that my level of self-efficacy was impacted by my race and culture. The work that was started by my predecessors has taught me that students in urban public schools are marginalized. As a black woman, I have the "privilege" of being part of the marginalized community. I have an affinity for them and am sensitive to what's missing. I use my race and culture to get access to pathways needed to close the achievement gap. These pathways include professional development, participating in teacher fellowships, and conversation(s) with other Black women educators. I put myself in spaces of learning that help to boost my personal and educator self-efficacy. Both my personal and professional efficacy needs affirming, as they are not exclusive of one another. When the self-efficacy tank that I mentioned earlier is refilled, I can bring a better learning experience back to the students. I also have the confidence to broach certain racially sensitive topics that impact the students' lives; supporting the narrative that black children need more black teachers. While this may seem offensive to some I want to simply highlight the fact that my unique make up adds to my self-efficacy and experiences. Leveraging our blackness - using who we are - adds a level of empathy because they look like my family members. I have the confidence to discuss what my white counterparts don't, won't, or can't find the words for: gun violence, police brutality, disparities in healthcare or education. My blackness negates the cultural mismatch that creates a barrier between student and teacher. Great historians and educators before me, like Carter G. Woodson, Marva Collins, Marcus Garvey, Mary McLeod Bethune and Fanny Jackson Coppin have discussed how the strong will and beliefs (self-efficacy) of Black educators was necessary to persevere through racially oppressive educational systems and tumultuous odds from the post Civil War era to the present. These odds were meant to confound the continued academic and social success in Black communities. Marva Collins, inspirational educator, demonstrated the highest level of teacher self-efficacy. As early as the 1960s, Collins taught in the Chicago Public Schools. By 1975, she set out to be a superior alternative to the failing Chicago school system by, above all things, assessing the self-efficacy levels of the teachers. Collins and her teachers understood that higher self-efficacy in their pedagogy would affect their perseverance in teaching, their level of commitment for teaching, and the goals they set for their students labeled "non-teachable." Efficacy researchers, Milner & Woolfolk-Hoy (2003) wrote, "...efficacy beliefs influence teachers' persistence when things do not go smoothly and their resilience in the face of setbacks."

Collins' resilience and her belief in the ability of her students to learn, using her personable and unique methods, is what propels me to say that Collins (and many other great urban school teachers) had already discovered that the key to her students' success was relational to the level of teacher self-efficacy that she possesses. She knew that in order to achieve great results that the behaviors she executed in the classroom were necessary for producing grounded, loved, and literate children. However, it was and continues to be the negative and highly bureaucratic course of action by state and government systems that continues to limit the development of teacher self-efficacy in large urban public school systems.

Drawing on past models and experiences are helpful in charting your next steps. You have the ability, but you are not doing this alone.

Self-Efficacy and Individual Belief

Self-efficacy refers to an individual's belief in his or her capacity to execute behaviors necessary to produce specific performance attainments (Bandura, 1977, 1986, 1997). When I look at my personal journey as an educator I know that it was my driving desire to be an influential educator. I believed, and still believe, that it is the professional duty of an educator to desire to create opportunities that will produce specific and positive performance achievements for our scholars. Distinction between the desired outcome and course of action is relational to the perceived level of efficacy that a person has for that situation. In layman's terms: If you have the belief that you can impact your situation based on the level and development of your self-efficacy then your desired outcomes (student academic and social-emotional growth) will prove positive.

Self-Efficacy and Social Cognitive Learning Theories

Self-efficacy is also rooted in social cognitive learning theories. Klassen et al., (2011) describes self-efficacy as the "confidence teachers hold about their individual and collective capability to influence student learning (p.21) A teachers' actions are influenced by the feelings, motivations, traits, and ideas of the children they interact with. The interactions should increase the confidence in both adult and child to believe that positive outcomes will be produced (Sainvil-Joslyn, 2021).

Self-Efficacy and Processes, Tasks, and Social Structure

My research also asserts that self-efficacy is developed through processes, tasks, and social structures that engage learners on multiple levels of intelligence in various levels of environmental complexities. Through the narratives told I was able to understand the distinctions of why behaviors and expectations are achieved in one particular area of an evaluation measure versus another. For example, the teacher that doesn't want to implement small group instruction for the sake of students being at the front and in control of their learning. The classroom, in sometimes the most lackluster building, could be the environment where students demonstrate the impact that and continues with what they've always been doing regardless of the feedback

Self- Efficacy and the Veteran Tenured Teacher

The one major advantage that the veteran teacher has is experience. Veteran teachers have years of access to students and best practices. In my research I learned that veteran teachers with high levels of self-efficacy are still willing to listen and learn. These educators still want and value feedback from their administrators. These kinds of teachers are high-leverage educators. As an administrator or teacher leader the goal is to gradually coach these veteran teachers to be future mentors or model teachers, through observation and feedback. There are always new instructional expectations so developing systems to increase the self-efficacy of veteran teachers will be profound. Evaluation tools don't always capture the totality of a teacher's effectiveness. Therefore, feedback from school leadership, keeping in mind how it's communicated can make a profound impact on the most experienced and willing teachers.

Quote from a Veteran Teacher

"A teacher evaluation does not intimidate me nor decrease my confidence. I often find myself making lemons out of lemonade when an evaluation could probably go left. If I perceive a potential issue arising during an observation, I will use it as a teachable moment and scaffold the learning experiences until I get the desired outcome. I am a confident teacher because I am flexible in my teaching methods based on the needs of my students. I also like to receive feedback on strategies that I could possibly do better."

What I learned during my research was that:

1.   Tenured veteran teachers have ways of articulating and demonstrating their experiences to showcase the attributes that enable them to have high and low levels of self-efficacy.

2.   Tenured veteran teachers want to be authentic stakeholders in increasing their levels of personal and general teacher self-efficacy throughout the teacher evaluation process and,

3.   Tenured veteran teachers' sense of efficacy are important to discuss so that they can grow their own efficacy and in turn, they may be able to be helpful to novice teachers.

Self-Efficacy and the New Teacher

The advantage that a new teacher reading this book has is that they are getting an early start at self-efficacy. It is critically important for new teachers, in large urban school districts, to believe in their ability to facilitate learning and thinking experiences for their students. For the new teacher, this will be the foundation on which they can build their own arsenal of best practices and teaching methodologies to produce better results in the classroom. The earlier the self-efficacy evaluation, the more students are impacted, the more confident the educator becomes in their ability.

☑

Chapter 3
Self-Efficacy and Collaborative Relationships

Joslyn Teacher Self-Efficacy Scale™

The Joslyn Teacher Self-Efficacy Scale™ (J-TSES™) was developed and adapted to incorporate Bandura's four processes that influence teacher behavior in different levels of task demand. The J-TSES can provide qualitative and quantitative feedback about an educator's aptitude to set and achieve goals and perform at proficient levels of expertise while balancing unexpected tasks and challenges. The J-TSES™ model assists educators in knowing how evaluation tools impact their sense of efficacy in how they use it as a tool to improve upon their pedagogy, ensure success on observations and evaluation, and more importantly, improve student academic and social outcomes. The J-TSES™ is a value-added approach as it provides a foundation for professional conversations among leaders and educators as they continue to grow their knowledge, skills, and abilities as an educator.

As I mentioned in my research, "These kinds of self-assessments and the teachers' own self-efficacy focus can also help provide a framework for teacher development training."

Collaboration with Administrative Staff and Evaluation (Collaborative Efficacy - Administrator-to-Teacher)

Developed for my study, the Joslyn Teacher Self-Efficacy Scale™ helped sift out what school leaders and future researchers need to understand; namely, it identifies the lived experiences of urban teachers. As I also experienced, teachers in large urban school districts are often cheated out of an effective feedback cycle and are expected to have a level of efficacy to persevere through challenging at-school experiences. School leaders have to first understand the process of the evaluation process and the implications of not properly supporting an educator.

Teacher evaluation measures are connected to the overall performance of students and the teacher. Therefore, when a teacher self-efficacy scale is used throughout the evaluation cycle, school and district leaders can get from that educator the depth of knowledge needed to develop and sustain practices of excellent teaching. Additionally, they can connect the subjective nature of how evaluation tools are used to the actual levels of efficacy of a teachers' performance. The teacher self-efficacy tool can support the educator by revealing the personal history of veteran and new teachers in themes and patterns on how their self-efficacy is "developed, sustained, and decreased based on situational, environmental and relational context" (Sainvil-Joslyn, p.60). In context to the hustle and bustle of a busy school building, school leaders will recognize that there isn't a "one size fit all" for measuring experiences. The experiences of veteran teachers can be maximized through the Joslyn Teacher Self-Efficacy Scale™ because it will broaden the opportunities for authentic communication and feedback from leadership. One of the most purposeful aspects during my research study was learning that "Communication and feedback from leadership are the administrative factors that the study participants' identified and described as greatly enhancing their sense of efficacy" (Sainvil-Joslyn, p.86). When I was out in the field (face-to-face and virtual) conducting research there were reemerging themes about communication and feedback from leaders that clearly resonated from the coding (finding themes and patterns in a data set) of my research data. What I found was that administrative support is a factor for educators as they shape their philosophies and develop their professional growth. Providing encouragement portrayed the school leader as empathetic and knowledgeable about giving frequent feedback. I want you to know that it will take a change-agent mindset and lots of tenacity to be the kind of leader that will develop and sustain pathways for learning for both veteran and novice educators.

Collaboration between Vets and Newbies
(Collaborative Efficacy - Teacher-to-Teacher)

The Joslyn Teacher Self-Efficacy Scale™ was designed to

give educators time and space to delve into deep reflection about their pedagogy. More importantly, it was designed to give teachers a voice. J-TSES™ can potentially lead veteran and novice educators to a powerful pathway of learning about how evaluation tools, such as the Danielson Framework For Teaching, impacts their sense of general and personal teacher efficacy.

Novice educators are equipped with the knowledge and confidence that they came into the field with. However, keeping the confidence up requires significant participation in a Community of Educators (CoE). Working and learning with veteran teachers can be a growth experience for new teachers by being vulnerable and exposing areas of pedagogical strengths and needs development. Through reflective cycles of discussion educators can identify the level of aptitude within an efficacy category. Then through these intentional discussions both novice and veteran are able to recognize their level of self-efficacy, setting and achieving goals that will improve their level of proficiency. Veteran teachers are the value-added piece to the teacher effectiveness puzzle. Through mentorship veteran teachers are able to demonstrate their knowledge, skills, and years of experience to their school leaders. Oftentimes, veteran teachers are either very active and take on school-based leadership roles or they are very quiet and passively contribute to the success and achievement of teachers and students. As experienced classroom practitioners, veteran teachers should be sought to support continued enhancement through the evaluation process. They can also benefit from understanding their evaluation process as it relates to their own self-efficacy; in hopes of being an integral part of developing and sustaining the collective efficacy among their colleagues.

I leave this chapter by noting that after an educator has engaged with the J-TSES™ that educator may need to make sense of the results. The power of interpretation couldn't be defined only by my interpretations. This work will take a team of dedicated educators who have the knowledge of their observation and feedback process, as well as the context and purpose for making sense of the results.

☑

The Research

In this section, we will share three of the research case studies from the original dissertation paper by Dr. Tracy Sainvil-Joslyn.

☑

Chapter 4
Nina's Story

Nina, 35 years, Grade 3-5 special education

Administratively/self-appointed Lead Teacher and/or mentor

Nina's Theme: Experience on My Side

NINA IS BEST KNOWN in her school and local community for the work that she does with her students' parents and families. Most of her entire career has been spent educating students with special support needs. Nina [...] has taught in a large urban school district for over 35 years. She values strong family connections all to ensure that her students are receiving the continuity of learning from school to home. Nina has a Masters of Education and Special Education certification to focus on teaching students with various academic and social support needs. She believes that her overall development as a special educator continues to evolve.

Nina described her self-efficacy as developing from her years of experience and states that she knows how to articulate to school leaders when her instructional routines during an evaluation works and when they don't. Nina described, during phase one data collection, how the Danielson Framework alone does not allow her to show her full teaching practice as she often has to explain to her evaluators the context of her instructional practices. The structure of her instructional planning for students requires individualized instruction. She stated,

> In all my years of teaching I have only once had a meeting beforehand with my evaluator or had a meeting afterward. After [one] evaluation, when I read the observation report, there were things that I was doing that the evaluator called out as not being present, and I had to explain to the evaluator that they were there, but they looked different from that of a general education class. After I explained, the evaluator understood.

Nina's experiences point out that without conversation, both before and after observations, the school's evaluation tool in and of itself can negatively impact a teacher's performance evaluation, which in turn could negatively impact a teacher's sense of self efficacy. Nina's story highlights the importance of the connection between the teacher and evaluator in building teacher efficacy. For example, in this situation, how planning meetings could be used as a tool between evaluators and teachers to learn about the specific classroom context so as to be able to conduct quality teacher observations. In the last phase of the data collection, Nina wrote about the importance of the role of school leaders in enhancing veteran teachers' sense of efficacy by putting trust in their teachers as they do their work. She shared, "After you [school leaders] have completed a significant amount of informal evaluations and you are certain that you understand what I am doing, then stay out of my classroom and let me do what I do and have done for [over thirty] years."

Based on Nina's self-reported accounts, her sense of efficacy is affirmed by factors not directly related to evaluations and observations by administrators. She points out in her interviews that her special education background and her instructional practices, in her opinion, are not aligned with the limited knowledge that most of her administrators have lacked in special education instructional planning. She describes how often the administrators that she works with would require an explanation so that she could teach them about planning and preparing individualized and small group instruction which can be completely different from the General Education curriculum. This is critical to my study because it highlights the inherent need for school leaders to consider, and find ways to learn from, the unique personal and general teacher self-efficacy that tenured veteran teachers possess.

Nina's Thoughts on Leadership Evaluations

During the second phase of data collection participants were asked to describe, the level (high, moderate, or low) and source of efficacy in preparation for an evaluation or observation, Nina said, "I wish I could say that I feel prepared for observations, but I don't feel prepared. I just do what I do and teach my students like I do every day and I basically ignore the evaluator and just do what I do."

Due to the special education assignments that Nina usually teaches, after observations, she has to explain to administrators how she is "actually" performing based on the Danielson Framework. Nina is highlighting how important strong communication and relationship between herself and school leaders impacts teacher evaluation and teacher efficacy. In a conversation, Raina (another educator we will highlight in a later chapter), particularly spoke about how valuable effective communication and feedback from leadership would be on her instructional practice. Nina also shared a powerful and insightful perspective on her own self-efficacy. She said, "My experience was around before the Framework and I always did what was best for my students. I have a great family of my own and student families that supported and trusted my work. That is my motivation to be better."

Nina, the longest tenured participant, with 35 plus years experience, also detailed in the second data collection cycle, how a new digital and virtual learning structure impacted her confidence exclusively to the "new ways of doing things" but not to her belief about being confident in herself and defending her experience.

I believe I am a confident teacher, I am a part of a new

program that has required me to stretch out and learn new things initially. Now that we are virtual, my learning of new things and new ways of doing things has greatly impacted my confidence because I have had to learn more computer skills that I had no knowledge of. I feel more under stress much of the time now as opposed to just being able to teach like I did when we were in a brick and mortar school. The stress is unbelievable.

To Framework or Not to Framework

Nina demonstrated the importance of understanding veteran teachers outside the parameters of The Framework for Teaching. Nina described her overall development as a teacher. She says:

I am self-driven and don't rely on The Framework for Teaching. My overall development as a special educator continues to evolve. I know about the Framework but I don't need it as a tool for demonstrating student success [that is used for her school to demonstrate student success]. My own family and my students' families play a bigger role in how I perceive my ability to educate my students.

Nina's teacher internal efficacy, as I noted also with Raina, is a strong indicator and influence on her degree of commitment to teaching. Nina's expertise and experience in the field, to her, supersedes The Framework for Teaching and the influence of administrators' feedback on her self-efficacy. When she was asked to describe how her self-efficacy for teaching evolved over the years, Nina wrote, "I am more willing to trust my gut in carrying out my duties." Her gut, a component of that teacher internal efficacy, is a viable factor for administrators to consider when working with and evaluating veteran teachers. Nina's trust of her "gut" is critical to her personal teacher efficacy because her "gut" is not quantifiable or included on an evaluation, unless she is given the voice to reason.

What the Self-Efficacy Evaluation Revealed

Nina declared that her self-efficacy came from her years of experience. It is important to note that Nina is self-aware in observing the evaluation methods used on her. She is clear that as a special educator, the rubric does not quite encapsulate the scope of her experience in the classroom. She says, "I rarely find the feedback particularly useful because they never offer assistance in improving craft, rather just pointing out what they believe are flaws. Therefore, I read over them, and where I believe it is accurate, I will do some research to improve my teaching."

Evolving as a Teacher

Nina says, "Veteran teachers have been through many "pendulum swings" of education over the years and the constant changes can really impact self-efficacy. Better, more effective, professional development sessions that focus on the how rather than the what would be a huge help."

Race as it Pertains to Teaching

Nina wrote, "I am an African-American teacher. I don't believe that my race is impacted by being at this school. I am secure in my teaching skills and therefore, I feel that my level of efficacy is impacted because of my race."

In other words, Nina is secure in her teaching abilities because of her race, and furthermore because there is a greater opportunity to forge relationships with the parents and members of the community.

What New Teachers Can Learn from Nina

Teaching extends beyond the classroom. In order for students to thrive, the teachers' relationships with the families are key. Although Nina's focus is in Special Education, this extends to teachers in general. No, you don't necessarily have the capacity to communicate with every parent and forge relationships, but this can be the turnaround for children who are considered at-risk. Sharing progress or concerns that may not be able to wait until the parent-teacher conference can change the course of the student's path. Of course, the parent has to be engaged. But sometimes, they won't be unless they sense you actually care about the child's success.

☑

Chapter 5
Harriet's Story

Harriet, 15 years, General & Special Education, Grade 6-8
Administratively/self-appointed Lead Teacher and/or mentor
Harriet's Theme: The Collaboration Journey Continues

HARRIET, A TEAM PLAYER at her school, is known for her strong commitment to student leadership and building professional learning circles within her school. Her students admire and respect her for the way she is involved in their community and in their lives. Harriet is respected throughout her school for modeling teacher leadership and civic responsibility for her students. Harriet, a certified teacher, has a Masters of Education with more than 15 years of experience educating in a large urban school district.

What the Self-Efficacy Evaluation Revealed

The Framework for Teaching (Danielson, 2013), as an

evaluation tool impacts her sense of efficacy with how she uses it as a tool to improve her pedagogy, ensure success on observations and evaluations, and improve student learning. In talking about her sense of efficacy she stated:

> A teacher evaluation does not intimidate me nor decrease my confidence. I often find myself making lemons out of lemonade when an evaluation could probably go left. If I perceive a potential issue arising during an observation, I will use it as a teachable moment and scaffold the learning experiences until I get the desired outcome.

Building Professional Learning Circles

When asked about what source (life, environment, professional) contributed to her sense of efficacy over the years, Harriet wrote:

> Experience is the best teacher. My efficacy has evolved from my early years of teaching. Those years provided me with opportunities to be mentored by experienced teachers, exposed me to high level professional development and opportunities to hone my teaching craft. I have learned through teaching and seeing the aha moment in my students eyes. I have a variety of teaching experiences at different schools, so I have multiple lenses to view a situation.

As she described in her response, her early years provided her "with the opportunities to be mentored by experienced teachers."

Mentorship can support novice educators in learning the steps in becoming an efficacious and lasting veteran educator. Importantly, mentorship is not a component assessed in the Danielson Framework for Teaching but it "may be used as the foundation of a school or district's mentoring...processes...helping teachers become more thoughtful practitioners" (Danielson, 2013).

This is important because veteran teachers can support and mentor novice teachers to help them develop higher levels of teacher self-efficacy. Both the novice and veteran can become more efficacious in their instructional and leadership practices respectively; which is the result of their cumulative experiences. In addition to talking about collaboration among teachers as supporting teacher efficacy, all three participants demonstrated this idea of being "thoughtful practitioners" when they rated themselves on the Teacher Self-Efficacy scale. Each participant self-rated to be very effective and extremely effective in the efficacy component titled Help other teachers with their teaching skills.

Collaborative Efficacy

As we discussed, collaborative efficacy comes from evaluation from an administrator as well as mentorship relationships. However, in phase one of the data collection process Harriet noted "the importance of time" as a hindrance not only to collaborative efficacy but to overall efficacy. She reported, "Time has always been a factor, not enough time to have effective collaboration with partner teachers" in improving her pedagogy within the Danielson Framework for Teaching. This suggests that time is another resource that is on short supply at underfunded schools.

What New Teachers Can Learn from Harriet

Harriet says that the self-efficacy scale "... has increased my awareness of my perceptions around the topic. It has inspired me to be more purposeful and intentional in my practice. It has also inspired me to develop action plans to resolve areas of weakness." Ironically, the afore-mentioned collaborative experiences are also a place where the new teacher can share what they know. New teachers may be aware of the most recent method of teaching subject matter. They may even be in tune with the slang the children use so they are able to better connect and share with the veteran teacher some of the new language that sounds foreign. They are also typically astute when it comes to technology that tenured teachers often find challenging. In a nutshell, everyone benefits from this collaborative union.

Harriet also noted, "As I develop strategies that work for me, I will share these strategies with my students to increase their repertoire of strategies they can employ as life-long learners." New teachers can walk away from Harriet's experience understanding that improvement does not happen on a whim or a wish. It requires a well-thought action plan and discipline that is then imparted to the children.

☑

Chapter 6
Raina's Story

Raina, 10 years, Grade K-3

Administratively/self-appointed lead teacher and/or mentor

Raina's Theme: Internal Will to Succeed - I Take Ownership

RAINA HAS BEEN TEACHING for over 10 years in various charter, private and mostly large public schools. Her interest in education and teacher leadership resonated with her very first inquiry about the study of teacher self-efficacy in terms of evaluative measures,specifically the Danielson Framework. She teaches in grades K-3. Moving in different teaching and leadership positions, Raina currently serves as an Instructional Teacher Leader. When it comes to teacher evaluations, Raina says:

> I believe I have a fair amount of control over preparation for an observation. I believe I have the control of reading through the Framework myself, pinpointing the descriptors that indicate "distinguished" from

"proficient" and then crafting my lessons to match the Framework. I feel the only source is reading and studying the Framework itself.

One attribute that educators can consider is a teacher's personal will to succeed or succumb to challenging circumstances. The self-efficacy beliefs that teachers have about their will to succeed are impactful and influence their capabilities to achieve (Pajares, 1996). To attribute her personal development to the steps that she takes in studying the Framework, to ensure that she ranks at proficient and/or distinguished by tapping in her in her beliefs of what she controls is considered to me Raina's teacher internal efficacy. Moreover, Raina tells us the power behind strong administrative leadership in helping novice educators succeed and remaining in the field; becoming tenured veteran educators.

What the Self-Efficacy Evaluation Revealed

When asked, "What life/environment/professional sources contributed most to your sense of efficacy?" Raina responded:

> I had two factors. First, I think it is just part of my personality. I believe I am in control of my own "destiny," and I thrive on challenges. Sticking it out through really tough years has allowed me to emerge stronger. Additionally, three years into my teaching experience I

worked under an administrator who contributed to my sense of efficacy. She really strengthened my beliefs that I have what it takes to succeed.

Raina acknowledges internal and external factors in helping her attain a sense of efficacy. She cites her own personality and motivating factors like endurance during difficult times. But she also credits a perhaps unofficial mentor who strengthened her "beliefs that I had what it takes to succeed." In other words, teachers need an internal motivation and external stimulus for encouragement and perseverance.

This is why a Community of Educators (CoE) is important for the engagement and growth of new and veteran teachers. This is why the community you choose to align with is very important. A colleague who only commiserates can be an added obstacle. So even though a school may lack funding for mentorship, there is a teacher or colleague in your midst who can be a sounding board, voice of reason, and/or cheerleader. This coupled with J-TSES™ is how tenured (self-efficacious) veteran teachers are formed and molded.

The efficacy model reveals that efficacy requires an inward desire and belief coupled with external support. The external support could look like coaching, principals and district leaders observing and providing feedback, and whatever else the school leader and teacher can hopefully agree will benefit student outcomes (for life!). There is a saying "It takes a village to raise a child." I would add that it takes a village to raise a new teacher and retain a veteran teacher by encouraging teachers to (continue to) believe they have the ability to succeed in raising the bar in order to close the children's achievement gaps.

Raina's Thoughts on Teacher Leadership

In phase two of data collection Raina detailed her experience with administrative leaders.

In this school my experiences are very similar to my experience at the other school I have taught. I was more or less left to my own devices to do as I see fit in the classroom with very little feedback or directives. On a rare occasion an administrator would do an informal/formal observation and I would receive very generic feedback (based on the Danielson rubric) with no advice or guidance for how to improve my craft. I am a confident teacher. Over the past 12 years I have learned that in my specific district the evaluators are seldom seen and often only capture a snapshot of what happens in the classroom. I rarely find the feedback particularly useful because they never offer assistance in improving craft, rather just pointing out what they believe are flaws. Therefore, I read over them, and where I believe it is accurate, I will do some research to improve my teaching.

She later suggests a better approach to leadership evaluations.

> Give feedback that actually helps, focus on the positives and then slowly work on one point of improvement at a time, rather than hitting veteran teachers with a million corrections at once. Veteran teachers have been through many "pendulum swings" of education over the years and the constant changes can really impact self-efficacy. Better, more effective, professional development sessions that focus on the how rather than the what would be a huge help.

Raina's advice to her school leadership is advice that one can put into practice when navigating a shift into teacher leadership. One may not move into administration or operate under an official leadership title, but might still find that what they've learned has a value that can be shared with the new teachers entering the educational system. One may find themselves on the receiving end of a new teacher rant. They may even witness something that can be corrected by asking the right questions, especially having been through the "pendulum swings" that she mentions. In an official teacher-leader capacity, one has the opportunity to share the self-efficacy framework as a tool to evaluate oneself.

What New Teachers Can Learn from Raina

Raina's profile describes a desire to want to be a constant with the students in a season of change as well as be a (help) in saving a failing school. The word desire is crucial to the children's success. One's desire to succeed paired with commitment to one's own sense of accomplishment and/or responsibility to the children and to themselves will define and shape the teaching experience and the experience of the children in their care. It's not enough to simply go to work. The desire indicates a personal, maybe moral, conviction that what they do matters. One must have a desire, even a willpower, to try to overcome the obstacles [of change, lack of change, class behavioral issues, poor leadership, hasty or underachieving administrators, lack of resources, etc.]. If one is capable of accepting one's shortcomings, clarity about one's desire and motivations can help to determine whether or not one is effective. The same clarity will help one decide if one should remain in the community. The deciding question would be whether or not their presence is to the benefit or detriment to the children. Though unintentional, a lack of desire and commitment is a surefire way to misdirect or even set children up to fail. The earlier a new educator is clear on desire, the better off both the children and educator will be. There is nothing fulfilling about working without desire. An unfulfilled teacher who has no desire is a lethal weapon and is more detrimental to a child who needs every advantage they can to succeed.

☑ The Conclusion

☑

Chapter 7
The Conclusion

Here were many events and experiences discussed in the narratives. What this book is setup to do is provide educators with an avenue to self-assess, self-evaluate, and reflect with practitioners the results of domain specific actions that fall within seven educational evaluative categories. School leaders, managers, directors, and other officials are charged with continuously finding sustainable solutions. That, within itself, is an endeavor that requires the strength of the universe. Since I couldn't bring the whole universe to you I provided for you four themes of focus that educational leaders can use to develop the self-efficacy of their school staff.

The four themes critical to tenured veteran teacher self-efficacy that emerged during the holistic review of data were:

- Feedback and Communication with School Leadership
- Teachers Defending Their Experience

- Time Plus Teacher Development Equals Change
- Collaborative Work Builds Collective Efficacy

What resonated with this data is the re-emerging theme that communication and feedback from leadership supports and empowers tenured veteran teachers. School leaders are then able to create a safe and healthy positive school climate. In turn, there is an understanding that learning with and from veteran teachers' experiences on how to build their self-efficacy is vital to this work. Simultaneously, the teacher is able to self-evaluate with the purpose of maintaining a safe and healthy internal dialogue that encourages and propels them to recognize their ability and show up prepared to effectively impact the students each day.

Knowing the skills and strategies, or lack thereof, that a veteran teacher possesses can inform school-wide best practices, leading to potentially a strong sense of both individual and collective teacher efficacy.

In conclusion, administrative evaluations and self-evaluation are tools that are necessary for a teacher to grow and mature. Its purpose, when done correctly, is to allow the teacher to see where they need to improve, how their race and culture impacts their teaching practices, how their predecessors fared, and how they overcame hurdles, and what new teachers can learn from others.

Meet the Author ☑

DR. TRACY SAINVIL-JOSLYN is an Educational Leader with 20 years (and counting) of experience. Dr. Tracy is committed to improving the outcomes of our scholars through supporting the development of training that will strengthen educator effectiveness and support school leaders growing their educators' capacities. In her last classroom position Dr. Tracy served as the STEAM Literacy Leader. She currently serves as a Board of Director for Riverbend Environmental Education Center and as an Advisory member to the Board of Education's Parent and Community Advisory Counsel.

Dr. Tracy's journey in Education began as a Special Educator in the NYC Department of Education. She continued her Special Education work and developed her leadership skills with the William Penn School District and a Philadelphia Charter School. Not long after she joined the School District of Philadelphia in 2016. Since then she has served in various teaching and teacher leadership capacities and loves serving through community stewardship across Philadelphia.

Dr. Tracy is a native New Yorker. She earned a dual Bachelor's Degree in Elementary and Special Education from Medgar Evers College, a Masters Degree in Reading Education from Cabrini College, and a Doctorate Degree in Educational Leadership from Arcadia University. Dr. Tracy has centered her focus and research on Educator Effectiveness and Evaluation and Nature-Based Science via Meaningful Watershed Educational Experiences (MWEE). In her spare time Dr. Tracy indulges in writing, cooking, meditating, laughing and remembering how valuable it is to have time with her family.

References

Bandura, A. (1977). Self-efficacy: Toward a unifying theory of behavioral change. Psychology Review, 84, 191-215.

Bandura, A. (1986). The explanatory and predictive scope of self-efficacy theory. Journal of Social & Clinical Psychology, 4, 359-373

Bandura, A. (1993). Perceived self-efficacy in cognitive development and functioning. Educational Psychologist, 28, 117-148.

(this is its own reference) Bandura, A. (1997). Self-Efficacy : The exercise of control. New York: W. H. Freeman.

Bandura, A. (2006). Guide for constructing self-efficacy scales. In F. Pajares & T. Urban (Eds.), Self-efficacy beliefs of adolescents (pp. 307-337). Greenwich, CT: Information Age.

Collins, M. (1992). "Ordinary" children, extraordinary teachers. Hampton Roads
Publishing Company, Inc.

Johnson,T., Boyden, J.E., Pittz, W. J. (2001). Racial profiling and punishment in US public schools: How zero tolerance policies and high stakes testing subvert academic excellence and racial equity. Research report prepared for the Applied Research Center.

Klassen, R., Tze, V.M.C., Betts, S. M., Gordon, K. A. (2011) Teacher Efficacy Research 1998-2009: Signs of progress or unfulfilled promise? Educational Psychology Review 23, 21-43. https://doi.org/10.1007/s10648-010-9141-8

Milner, H.R., and Woolfolk Hoy, A. (2003). Teacher self-efficacy and retaining talented teachers: A case study of an African American teacher. Teach. Teach. Educ. 19, 263-276.

Pajares, F. (1996). Self-efficacy beliefs in academic settings. Review of Educational Research, 66, 533-578. Retrieved from https://doi.org/10.3102/00346543066004543

Pennsylvania Department of Education. (n.d.). A-TSI Schools. https://www.education.pa.gov/K-12/ESSA/ESSAReportCard/AMD/Pages/A-TSI-Schools.aspx#:~:text=Like%20Comprehensive%20Support%20and%20Improvement,at%20least%20one%20additional%20indicator

Sainvil-Joslyn, T. (2021). Harnessing the power of veteran educators as stakeholders in the evaluation process to advance teacher efficacy [Unpublished doctoral dissertation]. Arcadia University.

The Danielson Group (2013). The Framework for Teaching Evaluation Instrument. Retrieved on 7/2/19.
https://danielsongroup.org/downloads/2013-framework-teaching-evaluation-instrument